Bedtime Prayers

with Lolli & Pops

Written by Cheryl Kacal

Illustrated by Caitlin McGregor

- **Book Cover by Caitlin McGregor**
- **Illustrations by Caitlin McGregor**

Written by Cheryl Kacal

Be kind and compassionate to one another, forgiving each other, just as in Christ God forgave you.
Ephesians 4:32

To Landon, for making me a Lolli. You filled a place in my heart that I didn't even know existed. I want you to know that even though we may be miles apart, we will always be close in heart.
Cheryl Kacal aka Lolli

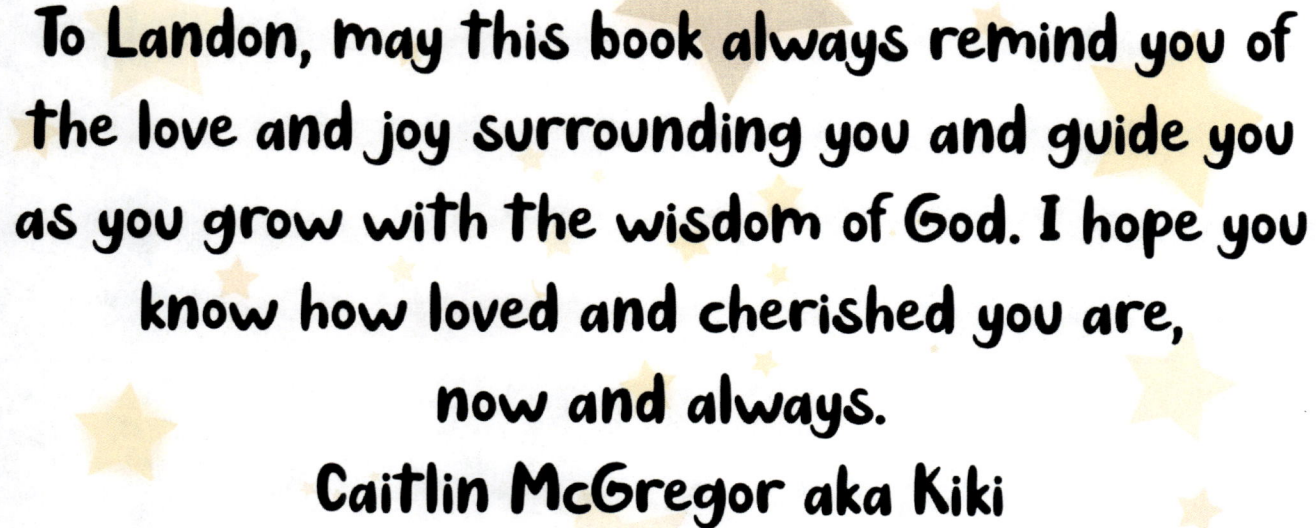

To Landon, may this book always remind you of the love and joy surrounding you and guide you as you grow with the wisdom of God. I hope you know how loved and cherished you are, now and always.
Caitlin McGregor aka Kiki

Lolli Pop's prayer: "Dear God, thank you for Mommy and Daddy's love that grew our family. Amen."

Lolli and Pops pray every night
for Mommy and Daddy's love
to continue to grow and shine bright.

The day your mommy and daddy
shared their good news,
Lolli shouted and clapped!
Surprised Pops starred at your sweet
picture he just unwrapped!

Lolli Pop's prayer: "Dear God, thank you for Mommy, Daddy, and me. Amen."

Lolli Pop's prayer: "Dear God, thank you for our love and laughter. Amen."

Mommy and Daddy are very proud to watch you smile and be so funny.

Now here you are, cute as a button and sweet as honey!

Lolli Pop's prayer: "Dear God, thank you for your beautiful outdoors. Amen."

Pops will take you by the hand, and show you all around the land.
You'll go hunting, fishing, boating, and so much more.
It's so fun to explore!

You and Lolli will talk and share giggles.
She'll shower you with kisses, hugs, and tickles.
Together, you will bake, decorate, and drink ice cream milkshakes.

Lolli Pop's prayer: "Dear God, thank you for this life and for the fun times we make together. Amen."

Holidays are a special time
for our family.
Lolli and Pops look forward to
everyone being together happily.

Lolli Pop's prayer: "Dear God, thank you for our family and the love we share. Amen."

Lolli Pop's prayer: "Dear God, keep our family safe while we are apart. Amen."

Even though we may
live miles apart,
God will always
keep us close in heart!

Lolli Pop's prayer: "Dear God, help us to always be kind and love one another. Amen."

Each day when you get dressed,
Remember to be kind
and always try your best.

Lolli and Pops love you more than
peanut butter and jelly!
They look forward to a visit to tickle
your sweet little belly!"

Lolli Pop's prayer: "Dear God, bring us together again soon. Amen."

When it's time to say
your bedtime prayers,
look up to the stars and moon.
Know that Lolli and Pops
are thinking of you,
and praying they see you soon!

Lolli Pop's prayer: "Dear God, watch over us as we sleep. We thank you for the hope of another day and the bright stars and moon. Amen."

95706982R30017